Published in the United States by Beaufort Books, Inc.,
New York.

First published in Great Britain 1983 by
Webb and Bower (Publishers) Limited
9 Colleton Crescent, Exeter, Devon EX2 4BY

Conceived and edited by
the E.T. Archive Limited
Chelsea Wharf, 15 Lots Road, London SW10 0QH

Designed by Julian Holland
Picture Research by Anne-Marie Ehrlich

ISBN 0-8253-0172-6

Phototypeset by Tradespools Limited, Frome, Somerset
Printed and bound in Hong Kong by Mandarin Offset International Limited

GARDEN BIRDS

Jim Flegg

Beaufort Books, Inc.
New York

Wren

Troglodytes troglodytes

The wren epitomizes the birds in this book, all of which are well liked and live in close proximity to man. It even had the distinction, before decimal currency, to feature, tail perkily cocked, on the reverse of our smallest coin, the farthing. Given the slightest suggestion of a fine day, in winter or in summer, the wren is in song, its bursts of tuneful ebullience astonishingly loud for so small a bird.

The wren's popularity stems from its presence throughout the year in our gardens. Wrens cheerfully go about their business, unperturbed by our presence nearby. They spend a great deal of time busily scuffling in the dead leaves beneath bushes or in the ivy on old walls of trees, seeking out spiders and insects with their fine beaks.

The male usually constructs several nests, domed, compact and well camouflaged, made of dry leaves and grasses and usually embedded in a crevice or deep in ivy, or even in a disused gardening jacket in the shed. There are usually two or three broods each summer, often of six or more youngsters, so the wren is a prolific bird and well able to offset the heavy casualties suffered in cold winters.

The Wren

Bullfinch

Pyrrhula pyrrhula

Even an enthusiastic gardener would agree that the bullfinch is a beautiful bird, the male splendid with his scarlet breast and black cap, the female a subtler mixture of suede browns. Both sexes have a striking white patch on the rump which is so often all we see as they dart away into the bushes. But there is another side to the bullfinch character. Beneath that black cap is a sharp, slightly hooked beak, ideal for nipping off whole buds from trees and shrubs and biting out the nutritious core. This process is so lightning-fast that blackcurrant buds can be husked and devoured at a staggering rate of thirty a minute, and those of popular ornamental shrubs like forsythia even faster. The bullfinch has had a price on its head since Elizabethan times. The chroniclers noted that 'one penny reward' was on offer for 'everie Bullfynche or other Byrde that devoureth the blowthe of fruit', so incensed were the fruitgrowers of the time at the damage bullfinches caused during the winter months.

During the nesting season, the male is rarely far from his female's side, often singing his soft wheezy song, which sounds like a gently creaking gate and is quite different from the penetrating whistle both birds use to keep in touch in dense undergrowth. They collect food together, too, carrying it back in hamster-like cheek pouches to feed their brood in a nest usually set in the heart of a prickly bush.

Great Spotted Woodpecker

Dendrocopus major

Great spotted woodpeckers have a harsh sharp call, but far more often they draw attention to themselves by bursts of drumming. Acrimonious debate raged among naturalists for many years whether this noise, like the sound of a kettle drum, was made vocally or mechanically. It is in fact mechanical, the male choosing a branch, often dead, with suitably resonant properties and hammering it with its beak to proclaim his territorial boundary.

As woodpeckers also use their beaks as a combination hammer and chisel to excavate a nest hole and to dig insects out of bark or timber, it is something of a mystery why they do not suffer from a constant splitting headache. Perhaps their salvation is a cushion of shock-absorbing tissue between the beak and skull. Great spotted woodpeckers have a tongue that can be protruded for several inches, armed with a barbed horny tip like a harpoon. Having cut into the wood, the woodpecker stabs its insect prey with its tongue and drags it out of its tunnel.

They are versatile feeders, eating nuts which they chisel open in the natural vice of a crack in the bark, and they are not averse to snatching the occasional nestling tit from its hole and devouring it. They are regular bird-table visitors, fond of nuts and suet, and even chopping through the suspending string to drop a tempting morsel to the ground, where it can be grabbed more easily.

Song Thrush

Turdus philomelos

Song thrushes are present in the garden all the year round, often coming as close to the fork to take a worm as a robin. In winter, our resident birds are augmented by wilder birds from the north, and it is these that are often to be seen dotted across damp meadows, taking berries from the garden only during the severest weather. In summer, when dry soils make worm-finding more difficult, the song thrush exploits an unusual food source, snails. They have developed the technique of smashing open snail shells, often selecting a particular section of the garden path or a suitable large stone to use as an 'anvil'. On this the shell is hammered apart, and thrush anvils are easily recognized by the multi-coloured litter of snail shell fragments surrounding them.

Robert Browning wrote:

That's the wise thrush; he sings each song twice over,
Lest you should think he never could recapture
The first fine careless rapture!

Although rarely so precise as Browning suggests, this repetition of simple fluting phrases two or three times in succession helps greatly in identifying the song thrush and distinguishing it from the blackbird.

Blackbird

Turdus merula

The blackbird is one of the most widespread of our breeding birds, and is a contender for the title of 'most numerous British bird' with a breeding population estimated at seven million pairs. Many birdwatchers would rate its fluting song amongst their 'Top Ten' favourites, even excelling the nightingale's. Most people can enjoy blackbirds singing, and can watch them go about their daily lives close to the house. Neighbouring males, each puffed up with his own importance and looking intimidating, pace up and down for hours, sometimes days, on opposite sides of an imaginary line across the garden separating their territories.

Although the colours of the male, jet-black body and yellow beak, are extremely simple, they can hardly be bettered for elegance. The brown female seems plump and motherly, with a homely-looking speckled pale 'apron' drawn up to her chin. An attractive feature of blackbirds is the way they live cheerfully and successfully in our towns, even though they seem distressingly often to fall prey to cats, or to hurl themselves fatally in front of cars while dashing about to find enough worms to satisfy their young.

During the autumn, British birds are joined by millions of migrants escaping from the snows of northern Europe. All gather together in the evening, 'pinking' noisily as they form huge roosts in dense thickets, rhododendron clumps being particularly favoured.

Dessiné et Gravé par Martinet

Robin

Erithecus rubecula

The robin, shown here with a bluethroat, a relative which breeds in Scandinavia, is probably loved so much today because of its tameness in the garden. It was voted Britain's 'national bird' some years ago, and deservedly so as its popularity extends beyond the garden to the Christmas cards on the mantelpiece. Its habit of singing in winter as well as in summer makes it even more likeable. The winter song is fragile and high-pitched, and stretches across the garden, like gossamer glistening in the sun.

Beneath a friendly exterior, the robin is a tough customer. In winter, the male and female set up separate territories, though sometimes they share common ground at the bird table. She will hold her own just as well as he, hurling abuse at any trespasser and chasing it off. As spring advances, her attitude changes, and a pair bond is formed with a neighbouring male.

Robins have always been at the centre of superstition, and in the Middle Ages it was regarded as sacrilege to kill one, a feeling perpetuated in the nursery rhyme 'Who killed Cock Robin?' These beliefs, and the robin's popularity as a Christmas feature, arise from the legend that it was the robin which attempted to draw out the nails (or remove the crown of thorns) at the crucifixion, receiving in thanks for its efforts a drop of Christ's blood, which formed its red bib.

2.
1.

Swift

Apus apus

In the past, swifts earned the name Devil Birds because of their all-black plumage and unearthly screeching cries. In summer, gangs of swifts sweep through the streets of the older parts of town, flying flat out, risking life and limb in collisions with vehicles and telephone wires. Doubtless swifts used to nest in cracks in cliffs, caves and hollow trees as their relatives do now in distant parts of the world. Now, throughout Europe, they are confirmed city dwellers, breeding under the eaves, and few birds can have benefited more from the spread of urban man.

Swifts, one of which is shown here with a house martin, are the most aerial of British birds. They sleep, feed and even mate on the wing. Swifts have been clocked in excess of sixty mph, and we know that they can climb thousands of feet to roost on the wing, or in search of the minute flying insects that are their food. Although the beak may appear tiny from the outside, it is capable of gaping open literally from ear to ear, becoming an effective flying insect net. The oldest swift that is known lived sixteen years, and must have had a lifetime mileage exceeding four million miles, because of its annual migration to spend the winter over the jungles of central Africa.

1.
2.

House Sparrow

Passer domesticus

The house sparrow, painted here with its country cousin, the tree sparrow, must be the most familiar of British birds, always closely associated with man and his buildings. It cannot be seen up in the hills or out on the open marsh or moor but it is attracted to occupied farm buildings because of the shelter and food supply which is provided.

Some sparrows have even gone so far as to decide that outdoor life is no longer necessary, living, for example, in main-line railway stations. Large grain stores and factories have indoor populations of sparrows, tempted by the offerings of titbits from the lunch boxes of the workforce.

Sparrows flock to cornfields at harvest time causing heavy damage. Gardeners also suffer: food is put out for the birds, they eat it and then start to tear apart crocus and primula flowers. Although this may seem to be sheer vandalism, it is not so. The yellow colour in flowers is associated with a rich supply of nectar (yellow crocuses have far more than purple ones) and it is this nectar at the base of the flowers which the house sparrows are seeking.

Goldfinch

Carduelis carduelis

The sparkling of the harlequin colours of goldfinches as they move between the thistle-heads in late summer is a clue to the origin of the collective noun for a group of goldfinches: a charm. The word could apply equally well to the song, a few notes to clear the throat preceding an extended tinkling trill. A bird which is so attractive to the human eye and ear runs the risk of its beauty being its own undoing. Tragically, for the goldfinch, this is indeed the case. Tens of thousands of goldfinches are trapped and caged on the Continent each year, and the same was true in Britain until quite recently. Despite the strenuous efforts of the Royal Society for the Protection of Birds, in Britain even now an illegal and unsavoury black-market bird-catching trade persists.

Goldfinches are birds of rough ground and scrub, and penetrate our gardens most often in autumn and winter in search of seeds. Many are young birds, lacking the bright head colours of the adults which appear during the autumn moult. They use the slender tips of their beaks like a pair of tweezers to extract seeds from plants protected so well by their prickles that other finches cannot tackle them. The sight of a group of goldfinches looking like jewels among the teazels, or disturbing the thistledown to blow away on the wind, has few equals.

Blue Tit

Parus caeruleus

Blue tits are the most agile feeders among our garden birds. They have no problems hanging upside-down on swinging fat, peanuts or coconut, but as it is their natural habit to feed at the ends of twigs, this is not surprising. Most of the time they are seeking out insects when probing around the plants in the garden. In the summer, they do a good job for the gardener by eliminating aphids and caterpillars, and in winter, when they may be suspected of attacking one's prize buds, they are just seeking insects or their eggs or larvae hidden in crevices in the bark.

Blue tits are notorious for their attacks on milk bottles. About fifty years ago, they learnt to puncture the cardboard caps of milk bottles to reach the cream. The habit spread quickly, and the change to aluminium foil caps posed them no problems. In many areas, protection with an upturned beaker is the only solution.

A man-made nest site often used by blue tits is a nestbox. Situated near the house, it allows you to share in the everyday life of the tit family: the house-hunting, the feverish nest building, the difficulty the female has in squeezing in the hole when she is plump with an egg, and the dull fortnight of incubation. Once the young hatch, life is hectic again, as feeding the brood of ten is a non-stop task for both parents for the next three weeks.

Jackdaw

Corvus monedula

Very much at home jauntily strutting between the chimney pots, the jackdaw has an unfortunate habit of building its nest *inside* the chimney. If the cavity to be filled is large, then the jackdaw pair add more and more twigs until the nest is large enough. A late spring fire will cause the jackdaws some problems, but more commonly it is the householders who suffer, because the choking smoke of the first fire of the autumn is blocked by the nest and fills the room below. Other more practical sites include cavities in old buildings and hollow trees.

The jackdaw has earned some notoriety for a habit it shares with the magpie of stealing bright objects to ornament the nest. As long-established urban birds, ever suspicious and alert, but at home inside buildings as well as out, jackdaws are easily able to enter windows with nefarious intent. Perhaps the best-known jackdaw is the one from Rheims, which (in the Rev. R.H. Barham's poem) made the mistake of stealing a ring from the Cardinal Lord Archbishop of that city, who reacted

> In holy anger, and pious grief
> He solemnly cursed that rascally thief.

Worse is their particular fondness for freshly-sown peas that can devastate the crop in gardens or allotment.

Nuthatch

Sitta europaea

Nuthatches, as their name suggests, specialize in feeding on nuts, although they do eat insects and their larvae, particularly in summer. Large and hard nuts are carried in the beak to a suitable crack in the bark or masonry of a nearby building and are hammered open with the beak. This characteristic noise is one of the best ways of locating nuthatches in winter. In many places, nuthatches are regular visitors to the bird-table, where they enjoy most offerings including fat. Tougher items like toast crusts will be taken off to their favourite trunk and hammered open in the 'vice'.

You could be forgiven for thinking that the nuthatch was a small woodpecker, whereas it scrambles about just as easily head-down as head-up, relying for grip on its powerful feet. Woodpeckers use especially strong tail feathers as a prop to support them on the bark but this only functions when they are head-uppermost.

Open parks and large gardens with decrepit trees attract nuthatches, particularly if there is plenty of beech, oak and sweet chestnut to provide winter food. They nest in natural cavities, often with a far larger entrance than is necessary. An oversize hole, and any other cracks, will be plastered up by the nuthatches in what seems an essential part of their pattern of life and which is a habit unique among British birds.

Spotted Flycatcher

Muscicapa striata

One of the latest of our summer migrants to return from Africa in spring is the spotted flycatcher. Very few arrive before mid-April, and they are not seen in any quantity until mid-May because there are not enough flying insects which are their sole food. The spotted flycatcher is ancestrally a bird of the woodland edge or forest glade, where there is a rich insect life, especially beside streams or lakes, although equally large numbers can be found in some open but much drier areas. They also inhabit places occupied by man: dwellings, orchards and farmyards where the chickens or cattle encourage a high insect population. Parks, churchyards and gardens are all used and the flycatcher is becoming a familiar sight in village, town and even suburb.

Flycatchers choose a perch with a good view and telephone wires are a special favourite. They will dart out from the perch, catch a flying insect (often with an audible snap) and return to the perch to consume the meal. The nest is often tucked into a climbing plant on the house wall, and may be used for several years in succession by the same pair, raising two broods each summer before departing south for the winter.

Blackcap

Sylvia atricapilla

Most warblers are sensible birds in our eyes, migrating south to Africa each year to escape the rigours of our winter. This is true of the majority, but the blackcap can be an exception. Blackcaps have never wintered as far to the south as most other warblers: many remain in the scrub of Mediterranean hillsides and few will penetrate south of the Sahara Desert. Now, increasing numbers of blackcaps are spending the winter here, especially in Ireland where the climate in winter is particularly bland, but also in the east and as far north as Aberdeenshire. It may be that a succession of mild winters, or winters with no really protracted bitterly cold spells, has encouraged this habit.

In winter the blackcaps turn to the garden, feeding on the juicy berries of ornamental shrubs like pyracantha and cotoneaster, and regularly visiting the bird table for scraps, where they have a special love for suet. Both male and female are about the same size as great tits and largely olive-grey in colour. He has the coal-black cap that gives the species its name, she a distinctively rich dark chestnut crown. At the bird-table they are remarkably aggressive; warblers should be tuneful (which blackcaps certainly are in summer) and peaceful birds. A series of harsh scolding cries, however, from the blackcap will drive off other birds even as large and as domineering as the starling.

BLACKCAP.
Curruca atricapilla (Briss.)

Swallow

Hirundo rustica

Swallows have one of the most phenomenal migrations of any birds. Each spring, they travel north from wintering areas in the extreme south of Africa, crossing tropical forests and the Sahara Desert on their way to Europe. It is a prodigious journey, carried out at speed, but at least swallows, feeding on flying insects, can refuel in mid-air. Today we put numbered light-alloy rings on birds' legs to trace migratory routes such as these, but marked swallows were used during the Punic Wars in 300 BC in the role nowadays filled by the carrier pigeon. Adult swallows were taken from their nestlings and smuggled out of besieged garrisons. They were later released, to 'home' to their nests, with a message attached to their legs giving details of the relief force's progress. Later, to swindle the bookmakers of the day, the results of chariot races in Rome were sent quickly and secretly to Volterra, 120 miles away, by tying threads of the winners' colours to a swallow's leg.

'One swallow doth not a summer make,' the saying goes. But how much more pleasant summers are for the presence of swallows around our homes, and it is often the same birds in consecutive years that nest in shed or garage. They arrive as early as March; stay throughout high summer, and in autumn congregate on the wires before they depart to face the hazards of the southward journey.

Woodpigeon

Columba palumbus

The woodpigeon is hated by farmers and gardeners in rural areas because of its devastating attacks on crops, particularly brussels sprouts and cabbages, during spells of severe winter weather. In sharp contrast, it has won its way into the hearts of many town dwellers because it has adapted surprisingly well to urban surroundings. Where woodpigeons have become established as common breeding birds in city squares, their muted subtly-coloured plumage relieves the sombre spectre of masses of sooty 'Trafalgar Square' pigeons. Woodpigeons endear themselves to lunching office workers by their approachability and ready, if not greedy, acceptance of any scraps of sandwich offered.

Their nest is a frail platform, made of so few slender twigs that you can usually see the eggs by looking up through the floor of the nest. It is difficult to imagine how such a skimpy structure survives the weight of two beefy youngsters, plus the added load of a parent bird when it arrives with food. Unusually in the bird world, pigeons produce 'pigeons' milk', which is not strictly the same as the milk of mammals. It is a white highly nutritious secretion from the wall of the pigeon's crop, and on this rich diet the young grow rapidly.

Rook

Corvus frugilegus

As much a feature of large gardens, parks and churchyards as of farmland, rookeries are usually built in the tallest trees around. Conifers, oak, ash or beech are all used, but over much of lowland England, rookeries and groups of elms always seem to be associated with each other. An old adage, suggesting that rooks desert dying trees, has a grain of truth in it. The recent outbreak of Dutch elm disease, which has mutilated so many England landscapes as trees die and are felled, has caused many changes of rookery site, and a decline in rook numbers.

The rookery is itself a town in the sky, with a community structure, and like its human equivalent, has its social problems. Older birds nest in safe, central sites but 'newly-weds' must make do with the fringe of the colony. Squabbles between neighbours are common, and the minute a back is turned, petty thieving of nest twigs occurs, so the rookery is always in noisy turmoil.

Any fine day with a fresh breeze will see the rooks over their rookery, throwing themselves about in the sky in aerobatic exuberance. Although much of this can be soberly linked with display before the breeding season, or with developing vital flying skills, it is difficult to dismiss the idea that with rooks there is not some element of sheer enjoyment involved.

Kestrel

Falco tinnunculus

The kestrel is our most common raptor, breeding in a wide range of habitats from farmland, woodland and coastal cliffs to parks and city centres. Nest sites include hollow trees, ledges on cliffs and buildings, even the windowsills of high-rise flats. Voles and mice are their main prey, although urban kestrels live largely on small birds, often augmented by lesser snacks like beetles and worms.

Kestrels have quickly adapted to hunting over the territory opened up in the broad grassy verges of our new road and motorway network. Motorways do not lend themselves to close observation of the kestrel's hunting technique, but this is well worth watching in a more suitable location. The kestrel hangs head into wind, its wings beating rapidly on calm days but with little movement in a strong wind, hence its local name 'windhover'. Body and tail swivel agilely to cope with changing winds, but the head remains rock-steady, eyes focusing downwards in search of prey. Kestrels will hover at a hundred feet or more, and with a marvellously acute eyesight they can spot prey as small as a beetle from such a height. With the victim in its sights, the kestrel plummets down, braking sharply, wings outstretched at the last minute, before siezing it in its powerful talons.

KESTRIL. MALE

Waxwing

Bombycilla garrulus

Waxwings breed in large numbers across northern Europe, as far north as coniferous trees will grow. Occasionally a highly productive breeding season, with plenty of insect food available to raise large families, will be followed by an autumn with only a tiny crop of their usual berry foods. In such seasons, the sudden shortfall in vital food supplies forces masses of waxwings to migrate westwards. This behaviour is similar to that of the lemmings when they set out on their occasional mass-movements westwards in search of food. The difference is that on reaching the North Sea, no lemmings can survive the crossing although many plunge in, but waxwings, with the power of flight at their disposal, are quite capable of making the crossing successfully. Thus it is that once every few years, east-coast towns in Britain receive an invasion of these supremely elegant birds during the autumn or early winter. By then, many of the rose hips and hawthorn berries in the hedgerows will have been consumed by other birds, so it is to the crab apples, pyracantha and cotoneaster berries in our gardens that the waxwings turn their attention. This gives us the chance to hear their tinkling trill, to watch their parrot-like antics, and to see at close range the red feather tips in the wings, like sealing wax, that give the bird its name.

BOHEMIAN WAXWING.

Tawny Owl

Strix aluco

The tawny owl, dumpy-bodied and round-headed, is the most widespread of British owls. Despite its nocturnal habits the tawny owl is well-known because the quavering hooting is so obvious and exciting, and because it has adapted so well to co-existence with man. Although primarily woodland birds, they penetrate into the gardens of suburbia and even into the heart of cities like London—anywhere with parks and trees and a supply of mice and sparrows for food.

Owls have always fascinated man. No wizard worth his salt would be without one as a familiar, and from ancient Egyptian and Greek mythology to Winnie the Pooh, owls have been associated with wisdom. In literature, references abound:

When blood is nipped and ways be foul,
Then nightly sings the staring owl—
Tu who, tu whit tu whoo, a merry note.

says Shakespeare, referring to the early start of the owls' breeding season. Hooting starts before Christmas, reaching a crescendo in February as the final squabbles over territorial boundaries are settled. Nests are in hollow trees or deserted buildings, as in Gray's *Elegy*:

Save from yonder ivy-mantled tower,
The moping owl doth to the moon complain.

TAWNY OWL

Great Tit

Parus major

The great tit is considerably larger and twice the weight of the blue tit. With a glossy black crown offset by a white patch on the nape and by strikingly white cheeks, it is unmistakable. The black line running down the centre of the breast is faint in the female, much bolder in the male. In winter it can tackle many seeds and nuts because of its larger beak and habit of feeding on the ground. Great tits are both inquisitive and adaptable and this has been proved by 'intelligence tests' which show that they can pull up hanging threads with a nut on the end, or prise open matchboxes, after first removing a peg holding them closed, to reach the nuts concealed inside.

Occasionally, perhaps once a decade, great tit numbers build up to unusually high levels after a series of good summers and mild winters. Large flocks are reported from all sorts of unlikely places like coastal marshes, and they cause severe damage to ripening fruit in orchards. Strangest of all, there are frequent reports of great tits eating the putty around windows, and even entering houses and tearing strips of wallpaper off the walls.

Starling

Sturnus vulgaris

The starling is one of the few birds which is as familiar to the city office-worker as it is to the countryman. Many city buildings have ledges that allow starlings to roost in shelter and warmth, and at sunset in winter, wheeling mobs of birds circle over city squares. Once perched, they do not 'switch out the light and go to sleep', but continue to chatter, a noise that accounts for the picturesque collective noun for gatherings of starlings—*a murmuration*.

In the fields or on garden bird-tables, starlings continue to be noisily gregarious. They are aggressive, shaping up to each other with features bristling, and making angry jumps into the air. They may be greedy bullies but their technique has to be admired as they are very successful birds.

Starlings are not choosy in the location of their nests. Any sort of cavity will do: a nestbox, a disused woodpecker's hole or, very commonly, under eaves of houses. The noise of hungry young in the early morning when the feeding parent returns to the nest in the roof can be most unwelcome. In the breeding season, the male is at his irridescent best as he sings, sitting bolt upright, throat feathers bristling and wings slowly beating, on a television aerial or telephone wire.

Sources and Acknowledgements

Comte G.L.L. de Buffon, *Histoire Naturelle, 1782*: p. 11, 13, 15, 17
Henry E. Dresser, *History of the Birds of Europe*, 1871–78: p. 45, 47
George Edwards, 1694–1773, watercolours: p. 5 (Victoria and Albert Museum), p. 7 (British Museum)
John Gould, *Birds of Europe*, 1832–37: p. 19, 21, 23, 25, 27, 29, 31, 33
William Hayes, *A Natural History of Birds*, 1775: p. 9
Edward Lear painting from John Gould, *Birds of Europe*, 1832–37: p. 35, 37
John Prideaux Selby, *Illustrations of British Ornithology*, 1833: p. 39, 41, 43
Title page: Blackcap, Robert Sweet, *British Warblers*, 1823
Eileen Tweedy took most of the photographs.
The publishers would like to thank the Council of the Linnean Society of London for their help and for permission to reproduce most of the photographs.